Living **Loom**

Threads of Life Woven into a Spiritual Tapestry

Prose & Poetry

Keni **Arts**

Scan this image with your QR code reader
for other books by Keni

ISBN-13: 978-0615603117

ISBN-10: 0615603114

Design, art & 3D modeling: Keni
Cover fabric: Peggie Davis
Portrait of Keni: Kenturah Davis

Published by Keni Arts Intl.
P.O. Box 207
Altadena, CA 91003

www.keni.com

Living Loom

Living Loom

CONTENTS

PREFACE

We live in two worlds; physical and spiritual. We experience the physical world through sight, sound, touch, taste and feel. The world of the spirit is one of love vs hate, good vs evil, faith vs fear, along with a host of other polarizing terms that describe its existence.

We find ourselves living on one or the other side of the 'tracks' in the physical world through any one or combination of factors; economic, social, political, religious, racial; and again the list goes on.

We *choose* on which side of the 'tracks' we'll live in the spiritual world by our words.

INTRODUCTION

Living Loom, *Threads of Life Woven into a Spiritual Tapestry* is a book of **prose and poetry**. The diversity of themes in **Living Loom** are as though spools of colorful threads were set in a loom and woven into a tapestry of spiritual life that seeks to connect us to God and to one another. The words are about life, even in the threat of death. **Living Loom** is a collection of words written on a tablet of experiences and beliefs that continues to challenge and transform me. With these words, I'll challenge you to consider your life in a transformative fashion. Here are some challenges that inspired me to pen **Living Loom.**

I was inspired to write **Haitian Train** after seeing news coverage of a mother determined to find her daughter in the 2010 earthquake in Haiti. The story is told from the daughter's point of view; a view that was born under the debris of a collapsed building.

The impetus to write **Pedophile Priests** came after hearing Miguel talk about the horrors of child sexual abuse committed in the clergy. Miguel (not his real name) was their victim. You don't have to look beyond the title to get the gist of this no-nonsense poem that shines a light on this dark, scandalous behavior. The *inspiration* came from seeing Miguel transformed from a lost soul to a free spirit at a bus stop in South-Central Los Angeles.

On the lighter side, you'll see what I'm capable of pro-
ducing when inspiration is off duty and I'm left to
my own imagination. **Busy Brains** was penned in
the middle of the night after lying in bed for hours,
unable to turn off my thoughts long enough to go to
sleep. The consolation was to turn a sleepless night
into a fun & off-beat poem with an ending from my
distant, not-to-be-repeated past.

Dedicated to:

my daughters,
Trenae, Kenturah and Tresell

Living Loom

Living Loom

The Lord's Loom

Our hearts spun from threads divine
woven on the Lord's Loom
entwine you in me
for eternity

The King and the Deaf Mute

The King sent His servant – a deaf mute
he panhandled scripture in mime
Quick verses he signed as commuters steered 'round him
as though he'd committed a crime

Some passers looked through him in disdain
an offense they cared not to see
Lace hankies pressed hard to their slight turned-up noses
so proud they were not such as he

The tempi of coins in his tin can
swirled 'round like a panning for gold
It wasn't for money he begged, but attention
to arrest a few weathered souls

As these searched their pockets for loose change
he searched in their eyes for a sign
That maybe this day they would see a great mystery
with their hearts and not with their minds

Beneath the dark secrets they'd buried
beyond the sad sorrows they'd born
His gestures bore wisdom from far beyond reason
to comfort, to heal and transform

He motioned for them to come closer,
then showed them a leather-bound book
The pages were old but the words were brand new
so grand they could not help but look

He caught much more than their attention
their thirst for those words were now whet
It was John 3:16 and Romans 10:9
the Word that freed them from all debt

Bible Art

Some folks have
a little art in their Bible
but how much Bible
do they have in their little heArt

Caring

You'll come closer to total freedom
when you can care less about
what *others think of you
and more about what you think of **others.

*God excluded
**God included

Pleading or Pleasing

If you grow weary of pleading with God,
try living a life that is pleasing to God.

Engage

Engagement with God
sometimes leads to
estrangement from man

King Fish

Sea of tall sails
horizontal hotels
provisional shipmates
at watch on the swells

God-sent armadas
itinerate tribes
cast out your fishing nets
walk tall on the tides

The catch of the night
shall live on in the day
we are fishers of souls
who know but One Way

Our Captain, King Jesus
too clean to stay dead
five thousand, then countless
from One Sole was fed

Deep Calls Unto Deep

The Word burst through the wails
conquered the clamor like a hammer paeans
from a tempered anvil He screamed
"Lazarus, come forth!"

Scribes bind folk tight in grave clothes
steeped in religion's cold traditions
Gray spun beards from grayer matter
ruminate they through pensive-less chatter

"Down through time we came to visions
dry bones breathe with flesh & sinew
But could one in his condition
truly ever rise i.e., abide again?

Why certainly we realize
though dead today, our friend will rise
in the resur…" "I Am!"

The Deep calls unto deep
at the noise of God's quick waterspouts
Praises swell – "Worthy" shouts the angels — sing
Rivers course beneath the veil; rent, void of sting

Drink the flood that hot pursues new birth
The Risen One shall spring from you

I'm drenched with rain of latter days
I pour my heart out that your heart's made new

God's Love For Us

I tried to understand how vast
the ever-expanding universe might be,
then considered that it would barely scratch the surface
on the depth of God's unfathomable love for me.

The Difference

The difference between being saved
or being saved and filled with the Holy Spirit
is like the difference between two television sets.

One receives its signal from a coat hanger while
the other receives it's signal from a satellite dish.

Painter's Pulpit

Preacher with a paint brush
planting trifold Gospel tracts
in the palms of passing people
those tasty Bible snacks

Jesus walked on stormy waters
He tread the dirt roads gritty
now He walks the trails of concrete
in this hardcore city.

The painter shares his gift on canvas
artwork comes from his heart
of all creation in the cosmos
you're God's greatest work of art

If You Will

Don't drink the far right's red kool-aid
nor take far left's blue pill.
Extremists views sedate ones mind
they'll make your heart go chill.

There's a place beyond what you
can see or hear or feel.
But first you'll need a second birth
it starts with just your will.

Will you take the Lord Jesus
whose blood for you did spill?
Will you give your heart to Him
allow Him to fulfill?

All your hearts desires and needs
free you from all that kills
If you will, you'll live forever
it takes faith, not skills

If you will, you'll soon discover
peace you can't explain
Wrapped up and sent from God's own heart
is love in Jesus' name

*How Shall We Do was written for my eldest daughter,
Trenae as she was entering her teen years.*

How Shall We Do

How shall we do in these blossoming years
spare the rod of correction, now dry those big tears

How shall we do as the dawn turns to noon
it's too late now for napping; for dating, too soon

How shall we do as the pigtails untwine
into curls and to bangs which are awning your mind

How shall we do, my child, girl how you've grown
yet in garments of innocence you've wisely sown

How shall we do since so shy we've become
just to touch one another in frolicking fun

"Here's how We'll do," whispered God in my dream
"dad, wait on the love of your soon-to-be teen."

Floored
Matthew 25:14-30

There once was a mister
who had a big floor
all shinny, fresh polished and new.

He packed up his baggage
and called his three peeps
and said, "I have talents designed just for you."

To one he gave five,
another got two
the third got but one and thought, I sure got src#*!

The first went and bartered
five talents to ten
the next flipped his two into four.

But stingy boy,
fearful that mister was hard
hid his talent under the floor.

When mister returned,
he called his three peeps
to settle the box score with them.

The first said, "Here's your five,
but wait, now there's ten."
the second said, "Your two made four."

Those two peeps, got much love
for their good success,
but what of the one who had failed

to take his rare talent
and increase to two?
Instead of engaging, he bailed.

The mister said,
"Fool, you fearful thing you,
you could have made bank with your one.

Instead you let fear grip you
caused you to hoard
it shall now be just as I swore.

So, give it up chump
to him who has ten
just look at you, now you have none.

You should have known me
and my generous plan
to bless those who bless me with more.

But sadly you're banished
to darkness and horrors
away with you. Off my clean floor!"

Busy Brains

some folks have hyper-busy brains
that whirl all day and spin at night
when they think, their brains are soaring
higher than a windblown kite

when they walk, their brains are chugging
like steam engines hauling freight
plowing hard, cold tracks of info
thoughts that most folks automate

things like inhale, exhale, heart beat
don't escape their tireless brains
some can even make their hair grow
just by thinking hairy things

few things seem to go unnoticed
by these folks with busy brains
"We're impressed. Tell us your secret."
"It's not hard, we're all insane!"

Come Together

I have a day job
my mind works at night
come Saturday morning
we giggle with delight.

Astro Rope

A jump-rope rhyme

Where're the Bot'ems, where're the Bot'ems?
Tell me, have you seen 'em?
Here we are, right here in
the Astro Rope Arenum.

How'd you get from one to twelve?
Do you walk or hop there?
On a frog, who said to us,
you really should't stop here.

Since you cannot stop here now,
I guess you must run.
Yes, before that crazy clock
goes "Cuckoo" at one.

If you cannot stop here now,
tell us what you'll do.
Grab the reins of Freddie Frog
and race Cuckoo to two.

If you cannot stop here now,
where will you then be?
On my way to grannie's house
before the clock strikes three.

If you cannot stop here now,
I'll show you to the door.
Thank you, 'cause I've not much time
to beat the clock to four.

If you cannot stop here now,
when will you arrive?
I'll be almost half way there
to greet Cuckoo at five.

If you cannot stop here now,
will you be in a fix?
Only if the little birdie
gets there before six.

If you cannot stop here now,
will you get to heaven?
Sure she will, chirped the clock;
once she gets past seven.

If you cannot stop here now,
We'll need an update.
Don't ask me, ask the clock
before it chimes at eight.

If you cannot stop here now,
you might need more time,
said the clock, but I replied,
I'll get there before nine.

If you cannot stop here now,
tell us where and when.
Here's a clue, there's the clock;
I'll be there before ten.

If you cannot stop here and now,
you'll go back to seven.
Only if the minute hand
beats me to eleven.

Maybe you should smash the clock,
there's no good rhyme for twelve.
Sure there is, said my cousin;
we'll stop at a dozen.

Thank you so much Freddie Frog,
you came to my defense.
Save the small talk, said Sr. Fred;
kiss me, I'm a prince.

Art Saved

I once thought
art was my salvation.
Now I know
salvation is my art.

Good Housekeeping
John 20:7

What was one of the first things Jesus did
when He rose from the dead?
He made His bed.

Living Loom

Introduction to Haitian Train

Haiti is the poorest nation in the southern hemisphere with 80% of its population living under the poverty line. The nation has no real construction standards, therefore, when the 7.0 magnitude earthquake struck in January of 2010, 20% of the buildings collapsed. Approximately 316,000 Haitians died in the quake; most of whom were buried under the rubble or suffered fatal injuries from the fallen structures.

As I watched, stunned along with the rest of the world, at the horrible destruction, I saw scenes of people looking for their loved ones under collapsed structures. One such searcher was an elderly lady who said she saw the market in which she was shopping fall on her daughter. Days had passed, and when the camera crew returned, she was still there digging through the debris.

When all hope appeared lost, her daughter was found and pulled out alive. I wrote 'Haitian Train' on the day of the daughter's recovery.

Haitian Train

Off in the distance came a rumbling sound
like a train come to visit our poor Haitian town
'cept we hand no train, nor tracks for the taking
still, in it did roar with a mean, violent shaking

Tin cans started rattling, glass jars made a clatter
they leaped off the shelf, at my feet they did shatter
I ran down the staircase, down one flight, or more
then off in the distance, I saw the front door

And then I saw sunlight, it came from above
I glanced up at blue skies where once the roof was
then darkness descended, it happened so fast
the building fell on me in a deafening crash

I screamed, "Help me Mommy!". She turned and cried
    back
from outside the building, she saw the beams crack
the weight of the timber said, "Here you will stay"
the last ray of light caught the freight train away

Trapped in the black darkness, but not all alone
a whimper, a sobbing and then a low groan
a shrill from an infant, a mother's long wail
inmates were we all, locked in this crumpled jail

From blackout of day came a nightmarish night
with dim hope of a rescue came fear and great fright
soon daytime and nighttime, they both became one
saw we no more moon nor felt warmth from the sun

As all thoughts of help turned to hunger and thirst
the presence of both said 'Prepare for the worst'
I searched the darkness, felt a jar not broken
it took all my strength and might just to open

What soothed my parched lips? Sadly, I cannot tell
Is this a jelly or is it hair jell?
But it did not matter to my swollen tongue
Since it knew no flavor, to moisture it clung

The loud cries or horror that filled the first hours
withered with time and soon died with the flowers
a jail mate close by me could whisper no more
while off in the distant came curses. They swore...

'God why not just kill us. Oh, why make us wait
to reap your full furry, to face our sure fate.
some called for the voodoo priests, witch doctor's brew
but they could not help them for they were trapped too

Then I heard these words of a rather still voice
So soft like the Angel, said, "You have a choice.
You must decide now to curse or to praise Me
Your words alone will condemn or set you free."

Then life seemed so easy while death seemed so hard
I can in my misery let down my guard
So I sang a new song, so plain but heart felt.
Right here in this prison, head bowed, my heart knelt

The song was so simple, "God I praise Your Name.
Lord Jesus, my Savior, Your mercies I claim."
Came God's ray of hope, darkness could not withstand.
For down through the rubble reached my Mommy's hand.

Tracts to Eternity

An E-flat blast detonated
A warning to motorists and pedestrians
that hustle had been put on hiatus
by a red train on the blue line
as it burrowed up to the Watts 103rd St. tram station

The barber pole draw bridge
held hustlers and bustlers at bay
on the concrete and asphalt mote
as the hot links screeched to a halt
next to the platform
one-stoppers hopped on while two-stoppers got off
with more distant commuters looking out

I stood by the tracks and passed out Gospel tracts
until the candy striped arms swung upward
to the heavens as if to give praise to the Highest
that more wayfarers had been handed
E-tickets: Tracts to Eternity

The Bridge

Some challenges and strife
may never resolve as you had hoped.
Here God may bridge the mote over which
He leads you to another walk in life.

Watch Your Step

Some people walk in the truth
while others stumble over it.

Soaring

A dream came true; I flew

I beat my wings against the sky
a mad and taxing chore

Till down I tumbled through the clouds
for I could toil no more

Then I stretched out my weary wings
the wind began to roar

God's Spirit caught, then lifted me
and I began to soar

Muse

In times of transition
and big decisions
turn off the bad news
turn on some good muse.

Get a Grip

You'll never start pulling down strongholds
until you take hold of the handle.
Get a grip on life.
Remember, your life is hid in Christ.
Can you handle it?

In the House

You might never be convicted
to the warehouse of law breakers
if you're firmly committed
to God's house of love makers

Ledge Living

nothing like living on the ledge
nothing like giving
'till you've got to pray to get it

Fun(d) Raising & Praising

less fund raising
more fun raising
all Son praising

Ozell

For my late mother-in-law

The air is still
save for whip-tailed cows
with hips twitching off flys,
ears itching, tongues licking out jowls

The air is still
save for a funeral parlor fan
on a wavy stick handle
clasped in a cotton-calloused hand

Soda pop
served in a Mason jar
to Mama Ozell
in a rusty old car

"Lawd have mercy"
she whispers as she
peers through dim eyes
into the deep starlit sky

Her eyes do skim, her
eyes search
the churchyard graveyard
to a polished stone; a shimmer

A double-wide
tombstone she'll share
with her sweetheart
no longer alone.

Her final farewell to us
then came a greeting
"Thank You Jesus"

God's Water Falls

I'd built a wall to hold inside
polluted rivers deep and wide.
The banks had overflowed at times
to drown the innocent and blind.
I'd destroyed what took a life to build.
Some folks got hurt...and others killed
The sediments of sin-seared-fears
fermented in a lake of tears.

But with one prayer
God made pure my spirit
made my shores secure.
From curst to crest
and brink to brim
new waters rose up within.

But still outside these walls remained
pools of my past yet to be tamed.
My head, my heart, the night, the day,
show me a sign, which to obey?

I bow my heart
God's Water Falls
on those who thirst
on Christ I call.

So soon you thought from me you'd see
a lifestyle purged from all debris?

It seems you thought the Nazarene
had bathed my body... washed my soul.
No! It's my spirit who in Christ is cleansed.
In crimson currents I now swim.

I launch out from the scarlet foam.
Christ soars inside me. I'm His home.

Not cold brute force, nor mild control
will Jesus use to make us whole.
For it's our will, our wall to dust
that lets Him pour His love through us.

Let's cast our cold heart off it's throne
'till all remains,
the Corner Stone.

The Peace of War

Like the father who lies awake
praying—listening for the footsteps
of his one Son from the war zone

I peer into the night watching
listening for the whisper
of Peace that sends all warriors whom

I hear His soft calling
over the thunder of war machines
A great blast!

A flash of light
cast from the blade of
a double edge sword

A knock on my door
I invite Him in
My long night has come to an end

Introduction to 23rd Hour

I left the keys to my apartment on the kitchen counter. Any of my personal belongings I could't fit in my 1965 Volvo P1800, I left there too.

Then I left Los Angeles; more specifically, Compton. I took the 110 Freeway north toward downtown LA, then turned east onto the 10 Freeway. I drove and kept driving. I cried, but kept driving. After hours on the road and eyes no longer able to make water, I thought I'd better decide on a destination.

Flagstaff, Arizona came to mind. I had passed through there five years earlier. It had impressed me as a pretty and peaceful place.

Now I was 21, escaping LA.

My sojourn in Flagstaff lasted only a day. The 23rd hour brought life-changing, even life-saving events. I saw a miracle.

Although '23 Hours' is written in poetic verse, it is factual; all of it. It was written in the 24th hour.

23rd Hour

What is this madness
how can it be
that wherever I go
the blues follow me?

23 hours in Flagstaff

Already I'm crying this song of disparity
the hotels and motels are filled up
the Y is my best bet
but even it says 'No Vacancy'

I'm gonna get my gun
I can't stand it
this is not how I planned it
I don't want this misery

But in that 23rd hour
came a soft falling shower
from clouds so low
I could stroke them; it's no joke

And in that 23rd hour
while the rain soothed my sadness
the warm moisture cleansed me
and bathed me in gladness

And in that 23rd hour
the sun peeked through the clouds
I stood in a light beam
around me a dense shroud

And in that 23rd hour
a rainbow before me
and mirrored above it,
a bow. God must love me

So put down that gun
I'm not crazy
my mind was so hazy
and filled with anxiety

But life is God's game
I must play it
and never betray it
I'll fight on to victory

Christ for All

While protestors take to the streets
to save brick and mortar from the wrecking ball

who will fall on their knees
to seek mercy at the wailing wall

who will not crawl, but walk the streets
who will stand tall, answer the call

who will proclaim Christ for all

Moving God

God's not moved
by the pigment of your skin
for it's the value of hearts
that gives us color to Him

God's not moved
by the texture of your hair
its your attempts to touch hearts
that stands Christ up from his chair

The Wisdom of a Mule

Sometimes the hindrances to success
are not lack of resources
but the abundance of
mesmerizing opportunities

Two keys to success
are two securely attached blinders

Stay Focused

Head Bangers

Let's face it, we're two extremely different eggs.
Since we're both in the same basket,
let's stop head-banging.

I Support

separation of church and hate

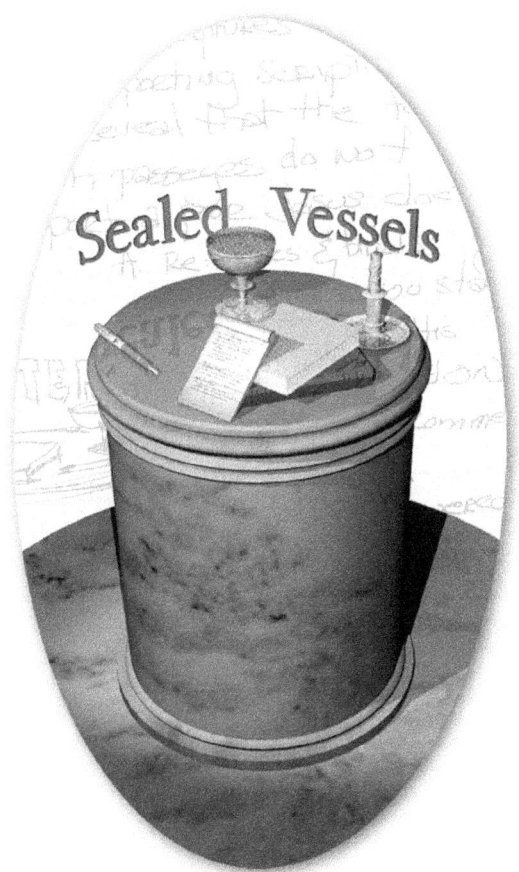

Living Loom

Peggie

For my wife of 33 years

On one accord
in the One Who guides our life
since I fell in love with you
and you with me and we with Jesus

Praise the Lord

I'm your husband, you're my wife
no such love has all the world
as half the love from heaven God has given us

Sure, we've faced some stormy weather
but we've walked the water
with our Lord & Savior

As our hearts stay calm, the calm will last forever

U Verse

UR-the-verse-of-me

Opportunities

When opportunities seem few
don't
hesitate
vacillate
oscillate or
procrastinate
don't even
hallucinate

formulate

help is on His way
so now
celebrate
God is

never late

Facts vs Truth

the wall of
facts will fall
under the
weight of truth

Giver of Gifts

The Gifter sought me
though I sought not the Giver
the Giver of gifts gave His best

He gave me Himself
when He gave me His dear Son
receiving His gift I am blessed

The Son has a Gift
great as He, the first Giver
not meant just for some but for all

This Gift is His Spirit
for you and your children
as many as our God shall call

The Chalice
For seniors

By God's marvelous grace
you've drank from the golden chalice
filled with wisdom, talent, knowledge, skills
and so much more

Now it is time to empty your cup into
vessels who thirst
to know what you've known
to see what you've seen

Then watch God pour into you
a fresh vision, a new dream
and fill you once again
and once again
to the brim and beyond
you'll overflow
once again

Sea, Land and Air

we have no gills but we can dive
no wings but we can fly
a wonder we can walk in space
a greater wonder is God's grace

Your Wealthy Place

Wild horses cannot pull you away,
nor will bull elephants push you in
God gave you the power to finish your race.
Now it's up to you to win.

Buck-it List

The young make lists of things
they will some day do in their lives.
The old scratch off from their list
things they will never again attempt in their lives.

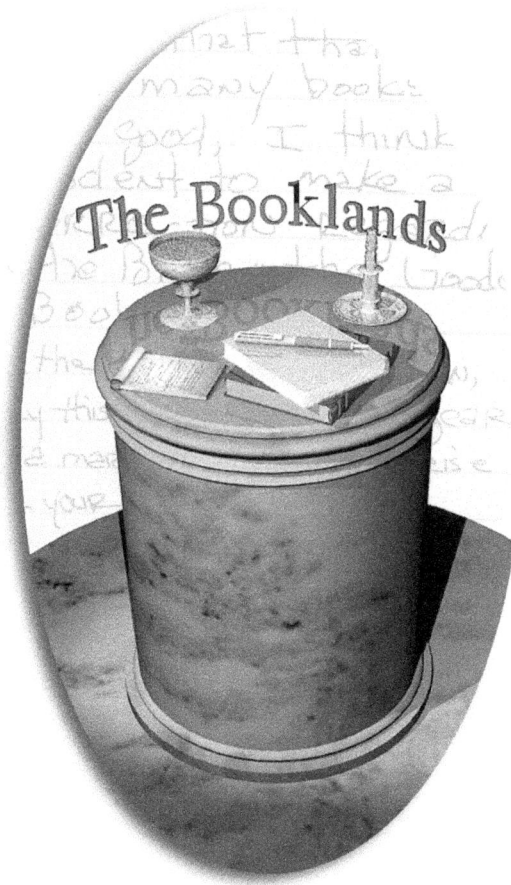

The Booklands

Living Loom

Ode to the Gutenberg Bible

A twister rose up one hot sultry day
and cut a straight path to the bookmakers galley.
It sucked all the type from its thin shallow tray
and flung it up over the San Gabriel Valley.

Then down through the funnel it fell with such force
that Gutenberg feared what might happen.
A lightening bolt struck, he shouted, "Of course!
I'll fire up the presses of platen.

I'll lay out the vellum and ink up the brayer.
I'll ready the presses for printing.
But first I must pause and offer this prayer
Lord, now let me do some repenting

For any past sin, whether known or unknown,
forgive me, I'm Yours to command.
The text that shall come fourth must be Yours alone
and handled with only clean hands.

The presses then rumbled and violently shook.
My joy I could hardly contain.
For I did behold the most valuable book
from which all could finally proclaim.

Was God's holy Word that rolled off the presses.
Full throttle I pulled back the lever.
Jesus' promise of life it addresses.
This message will roll on forever.

The Booklands

Inner in the city
beneath a particulate-laden sky
emerge from the ce-a-ment islands entitled, "Book"
On the plots of Book stand athenaeums sheltering liter-
    ary treasures
held in great anticipation for those fleeting seasons of
    procurement.

Among such are repositories which sprout from mani-
    cured lawns
and boast of engraved-in-stone proverbs.
Imposing towers fracture the horizon
vying among the pile for honor.
Footpaths paved in buffed clinker bricks and
trimmed in redolent shrubbery
meander past patinated sculptures and converge onto
a vine-covered colonnade through which
the sun beams a million spotlights
as on harlequins in a star-lit amphitheater.

Therein do patrician, plebeian and pedantic patrons
    promenade
toward oaken doors with polished brass handles
that summon their ingress.

Urban alternatives; aka 'book bunkers' to the homies,
crouch on blood and tear stained slabs.
Security-barred doors, over which hang gas lanterns
flickering to exhaustion
bekon to every passer-by along the walk of warriors.

Still, the masses on the mainland
divine for droplets of lore
in the craggy fissures of concrete
or on parched soil under an arid sky
infested by the demons of unknowingness.

We are neither deterred by ostentatious edifices
nor are we discouraged by unassuming facades.
We say, "Ha, ha" to the spirits of nescience
for we are life-bearing disciples
of the Lord of scholarship.
We go with illuminated faces and glowing expectations
and dare to darken any portal
that might yield the light of discovery.

Our passion is our passport.
Our currencies are bar-coded borrowing cards
of greater worth than any coin of the realm.
We come to seek sage reasoning,
to cull sound judgement.

We burrow beneath the topsoil of complacency
and tap into the moist roots of erudition
that we might sow seeds to the end of
Our Mission:

1. Return to our tribes
2. Bear fruit of the harvest
3. Lead them to The Booklands

So, to the highways and hedges we run
and solemnly herald this invitation.
"Journey with us to a land
plentiful of light-giving wells
into which you may plunge your ladle of learning
to unfathomable depths as to wistfully taste wisdom."

Come to the lands of Book (seemingly near heaven)
where voluminous watering holes
are bound in leather and lined in ink
on processed pulp.
Come here often, drink here deep,
for then you'll awake;
an ambassador of letters, an envoy le belle-lettres,
a minister of souls.

The Next Chapter

Almost anything
you want to know
is written in a book.
If your search doesn't
lead you to an answer,
gather all you've learned
and write the next chapter.

Ideas

A person without ideas
is like a hammer without nails.
They can't build
so they tear down.

Regulation

Information without regulation is like trying to sip water from a fire hose.

Inspiration

Information without inspiration is like a symphony of cymbals.

Moderation

Information without moderation is like a roller coaster without restraints.

The Goodest Book

Being that there are many books which I consider good,
I think it prudent to make a correction regarding the
    Bible.
It is 'The Goodest Book'.

Book Drop Box

The Bible:
Preferred by book-drop-boxes
at libraries around the world.

Open Book

An opened book makes a fertile mind.
An opened mouth makes a sore behind.

Jump the Shark

that TV show that you now miss
was penned by writers way too busy

writing shows 'bout missing people
jotting notes for their next sequel

staying up typing way past dark
for fear their show might jump the shark

Copycats

Filmmakers make movies
copycats spin sequels

Artists create paintings
copycats produce counterfeits

Writers pen literature
copycats cut & paste private label litter

Stagger Like a Drunkard

How were we marooned to the outer city?
they nabbed the gems we mined
then kicked in the beams we crafted
and pilfered the art we fashioned

But they could not take the songs we sang
those we forsook unwittingly
when it dawned on us
that we went wanting
for a most precious necessity

They took our books!

Except we read,
we stagger like a drunkard
across the intellectual landscape

Be You

The bold, authentic, brave, unique
these shall stand the test of time
But knockoff arts, however chic
are morgued with each day's news headline

Be Me

Is this mountaintop the place to be
if I like living by the sea?
Why cast my eyes on higher ground?
The beachfront is where my heart's bound.

College Bound

I don't want you to go,
yet I so want you to grow.
Oh, my, my,
Goodbye

Pointers

If you must
point at the darkness,
use a flashlight
not your finger.

What's the Use

the seed of a tree tells of its origin
the roots of a tree tell of its source
the rings of a tree tell of its age
the leaves of a tree tell of its name
the fruit of a tree tells of its usefulness

Thank Little

In the process of thinking big,
don't despise the little gears
that drive the big rig.

Leaders and Followers

leaders make things happen
followers get things done

Hoarders

How to tell if you're a hoarder?
If you can't see the baseboard in your house,
You're a hoarder

Living Loom

Pedophile Priests
Matthew 18:1-11

The priests in the pulpit were pervert
pedophile preachers of nambla
ordained of demons, they carried their gospel
to China, Brazil and Uganda

They spread their false doctrine in nations
so-called crusades were sexcurtions
alter calls made in the darkness of night
bidding boys to sex conversion

Those tangle-haired wolves in sheep's clothing
more twisted than wires in a cable
caught on their knees, not praying but preying
their collars pulled down 'round their ankles

A statute of law's limitation
allowed them to circumvent jail time
but one year to man is like one day to God
they'll pay for their crimes doing hell time

Trust breakers, youth takers, predators
their secret archives they have kept sealed
down through ages church fathers kept silent
now their dirty laundry's revealed

Gone from their net their catch flounders
tossed to the heat-simmering streets
left hook, line and sinker buried in them
so deep only God could now free

To harm a child following Jesus
the scriptures so clearly has shown
better that they had been drowned in the sea
their collar turned to a millstone

Miguel

You weren't allowed to play with toys
but you were made to be one
for men who turned God's house of prayer
into a den of treason

But with a whip of many cords
Christ drove those savage men out
and overturned their treasury
it was utterly a rout

Then turning with an outstretched hand
Christ now beckons to Miguel
and invites him back to the fold
where God's endless love prevails

Chooser or Loser
aka: Choose Her or Loose Her

are you more like Able
or just like the other...
Cain wasted the blood
of his innocent brother

do not shed your own blood
don't abort your kid.
you *do* have a choice
if he die or she live

your lady might shout saying,
"No, it's *my* choice
to give life or end it
you don't have a voice

it took two to tango
and now there are three
the third voice cries out
"don't forget about me!"

you should have chosen
to not sew your wild seed
but don't play your hand
with a far worse misdeed

you say you're a man,
well bro, this is a test,
to cinch up your britches
or slip on a dress

Introduction to Woman at the Water Cooler

For anyone who has raised children, it can be tough to take childrearing advise from someone who has had no hands-on experience.

The same can be said about relationships, especially the temptation to start one that might lead to one that would not please God. But has God ever traveled down this road?

The scripture state that Jesus was tempted in <u>all</u> points like we are, yet did not sin (Hebrews 4:15).

I recall reading the story about Jesus and the woman at the well (John 4:5-42). He was alone in a secluded place with a woman who had had five husbands. After a brief conversation with her, He told her to get her husband. I LOL'ed when I read her reply because I also <u>heard</u> her say in a sultry voice, "I don't have a husband."

Does Jesus understand the sexual temptations we sometimes face; if so, how did He handle it?

***Woman at the Water Cooler** is my 21st century take on a human condition that's as old as mankind.*

Woman at the Water Cooler
John 4:4-42

His flesh grew weary.
He needed to rest;
so Jesus sent His crew to bring Him back
a hearty meal and a tasty snack.

While the boys are gone
He said, I'll chill
right here beside the water cooler.
Then comes this woman;
He decides to school her

"Hi there lady, do you think
you could spare a little drink?"

"I guess I could, but with what?
You don't even have a cup."

"Ask drink of Me
and you will never
thirst again.
You'll live forever."

Then the lady said within;
this dusty road I've had to walk time and again.
But if once and for all he fills me to the brim,
I'll give it up to him...
this she thought with a sly grin.

Jesus, reading this 'ol lady
knew she's fix'n to get shady.
But before she could come nearer,
Jesus said, "Get your husband,
bring him here."

Now she really goes to scheme'n;
I think she might have a demon.

She's about to lay a snare.
She's up to some of her old tricks.
I'll toss my hair, she thought;
then lick my lips,
this works every time; men flip.

With a toss and a lick and a sultry grin
she said,
"Guess what, I don't have a husband."

At this point, I said, "Jesus run!"
Instead, he stays to get her won.

He answered,
"You got that right;
you haven't had just one.
You've had five;
now you're shack'n with the sixth son."

You might have thought Jesus had slapped her
with a red sign that read, 'Stop it.'
'cause she replied, "I perceive you're a prophet."

I should have known this was a situation
Jesus knew how to handle.
He wasn't about to let this turn into a scandal.

Seems that Jesus really reached her.
She went running back to town
and gathered men from all around
and said, "You gotta hear this preacher."

A few believed what she had told them
like young boys and really old men.
The rest came running just to see
if what she said could really be.

The men scoped real close Jesus' behavior
then said, "Sho nuff, he's the Savior."

Introduction to:
The Rose Parade
She Woes Parade
He Rose Parade

In celebration of each new year, people gather along Colorado Blvd. in Pasadena, CA to watch the Tournament of Roses Parade. The parade is also viewed live on television in households across the nation and around the world.

The Rose Parade tradition dates back to 1890. Another tradition sprang up in 1978. The Doo Dah Parade is a spin-off of the traditional Rose Parade. The Doo Dah Parade first took place on a Sunday, partly because the Rose Parade does not occur on that day out of respect of its church-going citizens.

Due to the highly irreverent, sometimes controversial and twisted nature of the Doo Dah Parade, it has since been moved far away from the Rose Parade route and to a different time of the year (April Fools Day).

Let's look at Dena and her sister, two estranged queens of two alienated celebrations.

The Rose Parade
(Youthful years)

Each annual one the people'd come
when Dena would strut her stuff
she'd parade her rose petals
but that was not enough

So she lifted some petals
revealed some naked stem
"Show us more!" the men cried out
was much to her chagrin

"More's not what you really seek
you really want much less
my lost and wayward sister dear
does flaunt her shamelessness

She's been known to bump and grind
men would shout, "Hurrah!"
then shock the horde to silence when
when she flashes her doo-dah

Her antics turned to madness
for she did it much and more,
'till even rubber-room guests said,
"She's twisted to the core."

She Woes Parade
(30 years later)

There was a time when men would come
to gawk at what she'd shown
Today Sister puts makeup on
in shattered glass...alone.

She looked for love she's never found,
now sees the years she's spent
in pacifying lusts of men
whose hearts were insolent.

So broken is her empty soul
she feels no one could mend.
She holds a shattered fragment
that will bring life to an end.

He Rose Parade
(Today)

The shards now strewn on dirty streets
reflect blue skies above
Then looking up through splintered eyes
she finds her one true love.

Jesus, mender of all hearts
brings oneness to the riven
Her dark past and gross misdeeds
in Him are all forgiven.

"I've waited all your life for you,
I heard your one last plea.
I restore what you've not had.
And you'll now reflect Me."

Back among the men she went,
the ones who'd hurt her so.
Forsaking fleeting pleasures that
they too may come to know

The Savior of all wayward men,
Forgiver of your sin;
Christ is King, the mighty God!
Do give your hearts to Him.

Living Loom

AfterWord

Living Loom

The Living Word

In the poem, **The King and the Deaf Mute**, two scriptures are mentioned near the very end.

John 3:16 states: 'God so loved the world, that he gave his only begotten Son, that whosoever believes in him should not perish, but have everlasting life.'

Romans 10:9 states: 'That if you shall confess with your mouth the Lord Jesus, and shall believe in your heart that God has raised him from the dead, you shall be saved.'

Salvation, aka, eternal life, is actually a two-part transaction. Part one was fulfilled when God gave us Jesus. If you believe that, you are responsible for part two. You must make a confession that Jesus is Lord (supreme in authority) and that God raised him from the dead.

If you're unsure of your standing with God, you can settle that right now. Here is a prayer based on the preceding scriptures. Don't just read it, say it.

Dear God, thank you for loving me so much that you gave your son, Jesus. I confess that Jesus is my Lord. I believe in my heart that he died and that you raised him from the dead. Thank you, for I am now saved."

Living Loom

About Keni

iArt for God

Keni is a visual artist and author. Many of his paintings are done 'en plain air' (outdoors). He has pitched his easel in cities across the United States and in Brazil, Germany, Mexico and the United Kingdom.

He is presently writing a serialized novel entitled, *She Can See*, which you can read on his web as it's being written.

Keni is retired from the motion picture industry, where he worked as a set painter and scenic artist. He also served as an art director for many years. One of his favorite pastimes is reading. His hobbies include 3D modeling and animation.

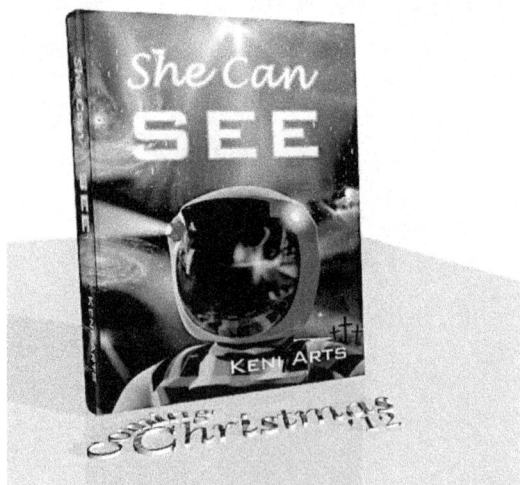

shecansee.com

Website: keni.com
Twitter: @keniarts
Facebook: keniarts
hollywoodbacklots.com

Special thanks to:
Peggie Davis: Cover tapestry

Keni Arts
P.O. Box 207
Altadena, CA 91003

Living Loom

Living Loom